EXTREME WEATHER

EARTHQUAKES

NorwoodHouse Press

JACK WILLIAMS

Cataloging-in-Publication Data

Names: Williams, Jack.
Title: Earthquakes / Jack WIlliams.
Description: Buffalo, NY : Norwood House Press, 2026. | Series: Extreme weather | Includes glossary and index.
Identifiers: ISBN 9781978576896 (pbk.) | ISBN 9781978576902 (library bound) | ISBN 9781978576919 (ebook)
Subjects: LCSH: Earthquakes--Juvenile literature.
Classification: LCC QE534.3 W555 2026 | DDC 551.22--dc23

Published in 2026 by
Norwood House Press
2544 Clinton Street
Buffalo, NY 14224

Designer: Rhea Magaro
Editor: Kim Thompson

Photo credits: Cover, p1. twintyre/Shutterstock.com; p. 6 Angela Cini/istockphoto.com; p. 7 Naeblys/Shutterstock.com; p. 8 boyoz/Shutterstock.com;p. 11 burakguralp/Shutterstock.com; p. 12 menur/Shutterstock.com; p. 13 Lina Mo/Shutterstock.com; p. 15 IrinaK/Shutterstock.com; p. 16 Christian Vinces/ Shutterstock.com; p. 19 Mila Supinskaya Glashchen-ko/Shutterstock.com; p. 20 maroke/Shutterstock.com

Printed in the United States of America

CPSIA compliance information: Batch #CWNHP26: For further information contact Norwood House Press at 1-800-237-9932.

TABLE OF CONTENTS

WATCH OUT!

The ground shakes.

Roads and sidewalks crack.

Watch out! It is an **earthquake**.

55

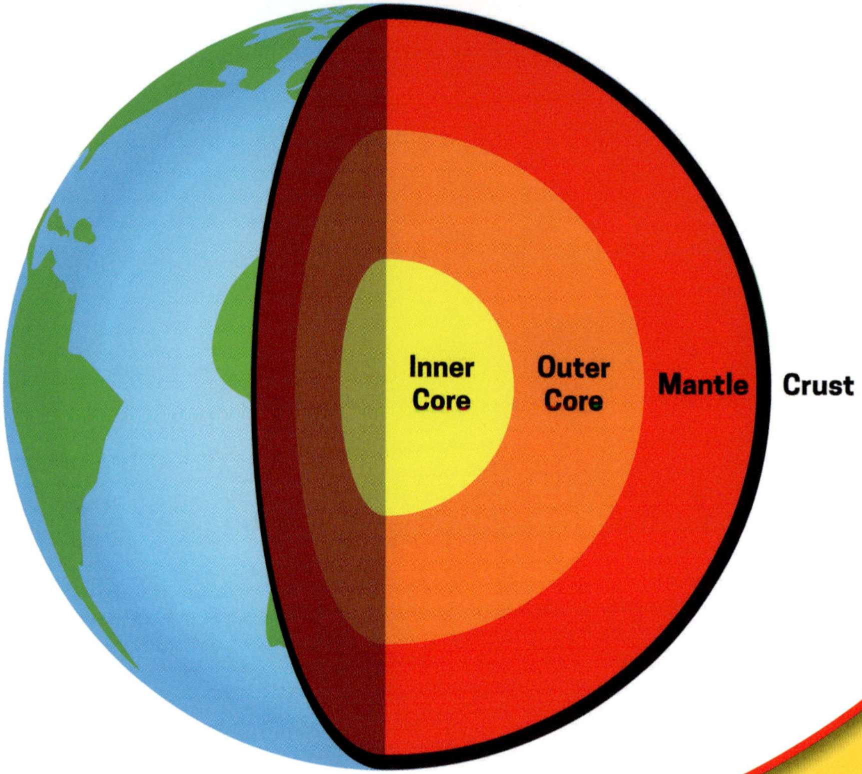

WHAT IS AN EARTHQUAKE?

Earth has layers. The top layer is the **crust**.

The crust is made of pieces called **plates**. Plates are always moving. Usually, we cannot feel it.

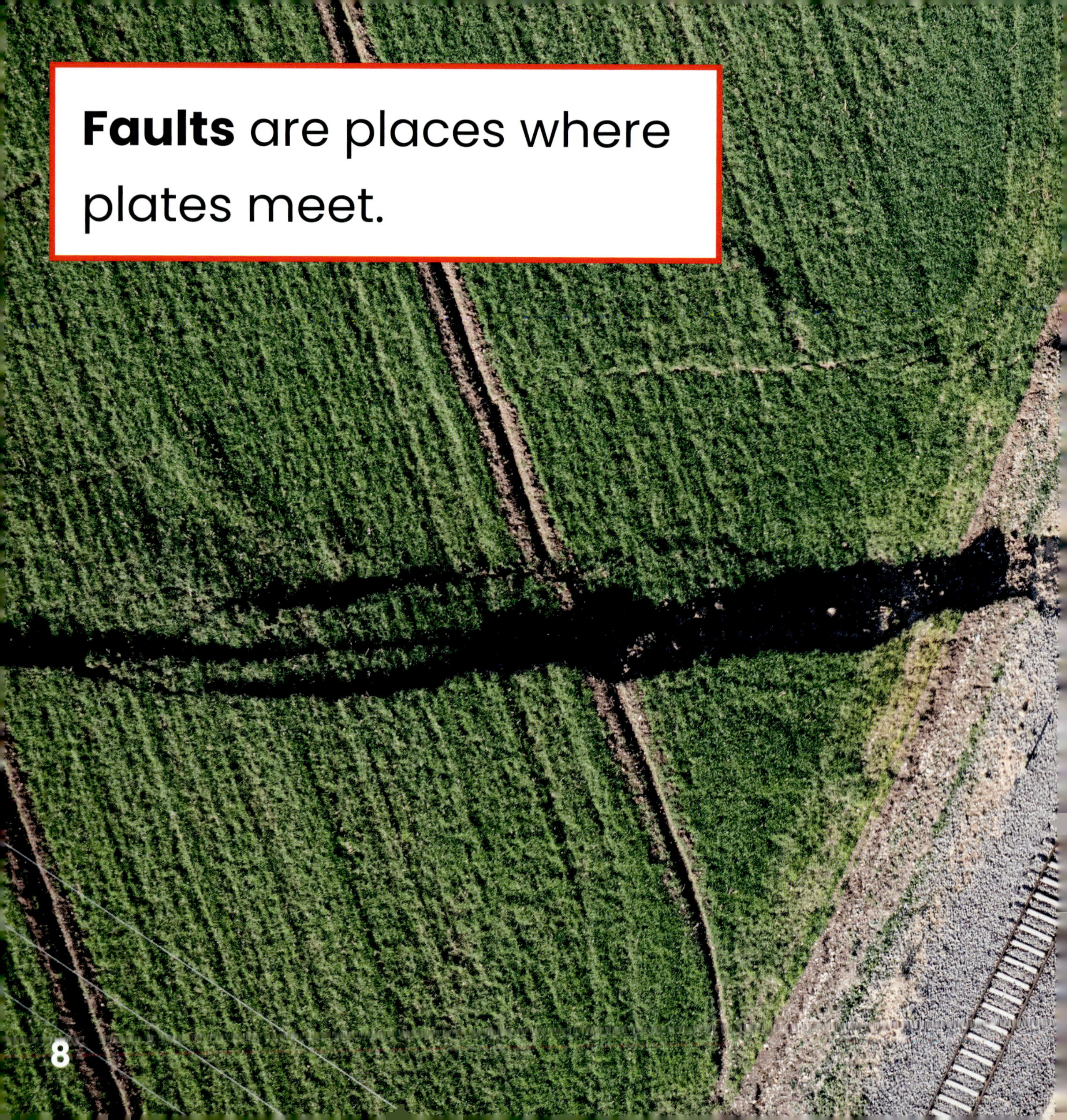

Faults are places where plates meet.

Sometimes, plates rub together at faults. They crash into each other. The ground shakes. This is an earthquake!

Most earthquakes are small and weak.

Some are big and powerful!

WHY ARE EARTHQUAKES DANGEROUS?

Earthquake shakes are called **tremors**.

Even small tremors are dangerous. They can **shatter** windows. They can break underground pipes.

Big tremors do lots of damage.

They can lift roads.

They can **destroy** buildings.

They can cause **landslides**.

Earthquakes under the ocean can make giant waves.

These **tsunamis** can reach land.

HOW TO STAY SAFE

There is no way to know for sure when an earthquake will happen.

Scientists **detect** small tremors. They warn that big tremors could be coming.

If you are outside, move away from power lines and buildings.

If you are inside, get low. Stay under a heavy table. Wait for the shaking to stop.

GLOSSARY

crust (kruhst): the hard outer layer of Earth where people, plants, and animals live

destroy (dih-STROY): to break something completely so it cannot be used anymore

detect (di-TEKT): to discover something or become aware of it

earthquake (URTH-kwayk): a sudden, violent shaking of Earth

faults (fawltz): large breaks between the plates that make up Earth's crust

landslides (LAND-slides): times when dirt and rocks suddenly slide down a hill or mountain

plates (playtz): rocky sections of Earth's crust

shatter (SHAT-ur): to break suddenly into many small pieces

tremors (TREM-urz): shaking movements in the ground

tsunamis (tsu-NAH-meez): large, destructive ocean waves usually caused by underwater earthquakes

THINKING QUESTIONS

1. What is Earth's crust?
2. Describe a fault.
3. What are tremors? Why can they be dangerous?
4. Why are underwater earthquakes dangerous?
5. What should you do if you are outside during an earthquake?

INDEX

ABOUT THE AUTHOR

Jack Williams is curious about all things in nature, especially the weather! He checks the weather forecast every day. He used to be a police officer, so he knows how important it is to watch out for danger and stay safe.